LIVE YOUR DREAM:

How to Set and Accomplish Deadline-Driven Goals

Liltera R. Williams

WRITING | PROOFREADING | EDITING | PUBLISHING

iWrite4orU Publishing
PO Box 551006 | JAX, FL 32255 |contact@iwrite4oru.com

Cover Design: Liltera R. Williams
Assistance from Omar Scruggs of A&O Design Solutions

Official Website: www.iwrite4oru.com
Facebook: www.facebook.com/iWrite4orU
Instagram: iWrite4orU_LRW
Twitter: @iWrite4orU_LRW

Table of Contents:

Foreword

It is with great honor that I offer these words for such a purpose-driven writer, Liltera R. Williams. I met this ambitious young lady at a writers' conference a couple of years ago in Tallahassee, Florida. I was giving a detailed presentation on self-publishing as she attentively sat in the front row. She kept slowly raising her hand to ask one question after another until our session timed out. I knew then that she was going to be a great writer, and today, she's a UBAWA and Amazon Bestselling Author. With a plethora of new talents releasing books seemingly every day, that's not an easy feat in this economy.

Now, she's publishing her fourth book titled, *LIVE YOUR DREAM: How to Set and Accomplish Deadline-Driven Goals.* Liltera epitomizes the title of this current book. From the first day that we met, she has set several goals and accomplished all of them within reasonable target dates. Not only is she a multi-published author, but she's also a poet, editor and publisher. She studied Creative Writing at Florida State University and went on to become Owner/President/CEO of *iWrite4orU.* As you can see, Liltera is a beginner and finisher of everything that she sets her mind to achieve.

The value of preparation can't ever be overstated. Therefore, I encourage you to read this latest book and add it to your self-help collection as a resource guide for planning your future. This young author is an inspirational leader with an incredible message for her generation and generations to come. With a poetic voice and keen intellect she can teach you how to set and accomplish your deadline-driven goals. Given her easy writing style, this book will not only motivate you to do better; it will show you how to be better, and live your dream.

Barbara Joe Williams
Amani Publishing, LLC
Author/Publisher/Speaker

Testimonials

You are BOLD, TALENTED and SMART and you make Mommy and Daddy so proud! As I was growing up I always had a fear of how my life would be, but I knew when I had kids I wanted to make their lives better. I'm still trying, but I think I have done okay with you and your brother. Writing was once my passion, so I guess that is where your drive came from. Continue being you and SUCCESS will come.
~Cassandra Williams

I heard you say you wrote a book. That was all the inspiration I needed. Please don't stop what you do.
~Kia Flow

It's through our conversations that I build and maintain the strength to continue to write. You are an inspiration through your daily focus on your goals.
~Roger Azul II

I've always loved writing and I have a notebook full of poems that I've written throughout the years of middle and high school, but for reasons unknown I gave up... until I saw your posts and statuses about writing every day. I became motivated and inspired as the days passed, but what really inspired me is the day I found out that you had your own writing company. I finally sat down and [realized] writing is my passion. I've been through my share of college majors, but they were just

interests, not passions, and I let them go. You gave me back my motivation to write. THANK YOU, Liltera, for your inspiration and motivational attitude that you have given each and every day. Thank you for waking up my talent.
~Angelica Edwards

You are definitely an inspiration to many and you have inspired me more than you would know. Thank you for being who God ordained for you to be. Keep doing what you're doing!
~Onyx Seven

You have a drive that few artists have these days; a "get up and go" attitude that is necessary when being an entrepreneur. It is very inspiring. There is no doubt you will make it to the top.
~Knight Krawler

You are an inspiration through your self-determination and drive to succeed. In the two years I have worked with you, I have witnessed everything from your modest ambition to incorporate a freelance writing business to publishing your poetry, working on your first novel, and garnering the support of the local media. To see you come out of your introvert writer's shell and perform your words in front of strangers is inspiring in itself, showing that you have the courage and passion to climb to the top. Keep working, branding, and doing what you do!
~Chantalle Johnson

You taught me that nobody has to believe in your dream for it to be real. You also taught me that dreams come true through WORK. I've been watching you put in long hours, sleep less, travel far, and write extensively. Your passion inspired mine. Now I'm living my dream as well.
~Bryant Cross

You have shown that Passion and Hard Work produces results. If you believe in something, you can achieve it if you really want it!
~Kenny Anderson

To me, it's more of the fact that you make me proud beyond belief. You came from where I come from. I know what you've endured and dealt with. For you to come out of it so beautiful, articulate, and driven puts a smile on my face. I wasn't around to see your growth, but I remember you as a young child and through Facebook to be tuned back into your life and see what you're doing now is awesome. Keep God First and Keep Grinding!
~Charles Felton

You have taught me there are no excuses! No matter where you're from, if you have a dream, live it! You have so much on your plate, yet you manage to make time for everything. Your determination is unmatchable and I learn from you daily. You have also taught me

that when God reveals to you your purpose in life, don't sit on it, begin to walk in and operate in it!
~Rachel Winters

Liltera, as a young lady, you have inspired me with your determination. You have not allowed any of your past obstacles to hinder what God is doing for you right now. I am encouraged to see you moving forward in God, and doing positive things in your community. You have shared some obstacles, but you have taken some advice and turned your obstacles into stepping stones. Continue to keep God first, and continue to be an inspiration in the lives of others. The negatives of life don't even matter; it's the positive outcomes only. Right here... Right now! God is blessing your life, and developing a creative and amazingly wonderful young lady! I am also inspired by a couple of statements you made in your book's introduction, "Amateur Thoughts", and I quote: "I am on a mission to spread love through language. Express yourself by doing what you love and loving what you do..." This is simply amazing, and today I am inspired by you to do what I love, and love what I do! In Jesus name! Thanks for being a part of my journey!
~Carla Hinton

I love your drive and tenacity. I am always inspired by young people who don't just talk the talk but walk the walk. You are walking my child.
~Angelia Vernon Menchan

I have learned that you can't live your dream only talking about your dream; actions put it all in motion. Claim it and it shall be yours! Thank you! No matter what anyone says, you are a blessing!
~General L. Lamar

Your drive, determination and tenacity are contagious!
~Valarie Holsey-Esguerra

You decided that there is no other option. You wear, say, and live it. You have given no plan B or fallback plan. This keeps me going, knowing there is someone else who just doesn't do it because they want to, but because living your dream is the only choice.
~Robbie Stokes Jr.

You have inspired me to LIVE MY DREAM by showing that it's possible through positive affirmations and setting goals. Your humble and perseverant spirit lets me know those are truly the building blocks of life.
~Sherry Blossom

You've inspired me to LIVE MY DREAM by showing that not only is it possible to do, but it feels good doing it. You'll [also] feel very rewarded, and be blessed while doing it! Your encouraging words give me hope when I feel I want to quit!
~Nikki Figgs

It is very encouraging and reassuring to see the words LIVE YOUR DREAM every day, especially when no one really ever said them to you before. Also, those words coming from a fellow writer is my way of thinking I can make it too. I can't thank you enough!
~Chereese Sheen

Watching you shows me that if I assert myself and take that huge leap of faith like you did, there's nothing that I can't accomplish. You are truly a breath of fresh air, and your #WriterGrind is definitely an inspiration.
~Riana Winters

Your motivational spirit reflects in your work and you have inspired me to complete a series of shorts that I began writing two years ago. You have also encouraged me to take that extra step and lose that hour of sleep to accomplish my goals and live my dream.
~drixLe

Introduction

In 5th grade, I was eliminated from the spelling bee because I misspelled 'entrepreneur'... and then I became one. While reminiscing about that unforgettable occurrence, I realized that I've always had a strong desire to succeed; I just didn't realize it until after I failed at something. The year was 1998. I was front and center, toes almost gripping the edge of the stage. "Entrepreneur," the announcer said. It was a foreign word, and the pronunciation was misleading. Still, I braved my first and only attempt anyway. "Incorrect."

I remember the overwhelming emotion of disappointment, the pause in time and, finally, my dismissal from the competition. As a result, I vowed to never misspell another word ever again.

Entering middle school as a curious adolescent with lots of potential, I wanted to establish myself as a scholar. About a year later, at age 12, writing became my new hobby, and again I was overwhelmed by a powerful emotion: loss.

Summertime was approaching and my paternal grandfather suddenly passed away in June of 1999. I buried the pain and searched for healing in between the pages of my notebooks.

Ironically yet fatefully, today, I can claim to be a successful **Entrepreneur** (pronounced ahn-truh-pruh-nur): one who organizes, manages, and assumes the risks of a business or enterprise (Merriam-Webster). Despite not winning the spelling bee, during my grade school years, I won other awards that validated my intelligence, including but not limited to: several A/B Honor Roll certificates, Super Seven recognition at DuPont Middle School and a Bright Futures Scholarship to attend Florida State University. I graduated from college a semester early and began aggressively pursuing a career in my related field of Creative Writing less than five years later. I am now the CEO of *iWrite4orU*: a writing, proofreading, editing and publishing company, Bestselling Author, Motivational Poet, Independent Publisher, Editor, Freelance Writer and the list goes on with various other associated titles.

LIVE YOUR DREAM: How to Set and Accomplish Deadline-Driven Goals is my fourth book; a non-fiction inspirational guide that follows two poetry collections (*Amateur Thoughts: A Personal Collection of iWrite Poetry & LRW Quotes* and *Words from the Write Side of My Heart*) and my debut novel (*Dearly Beloved S.I.S.T.A.S*). On February 17, 2014, after much prayer and planning, I quit my job as an SEO Copywriter in Corporate America and decided to focus on all that I am aiming to achieve, full-time. This book is the product of that decision. My dream no longer deserved to be a sideline hustle, so I became proactive in my quest to make it a reality. (Google #WriterGrind™).

If you are reading this introduction, it means that you are seeking an answer. Perhaps you want to know how you can find the courage to take a similar leap of faith. Or, how to discover exactly what it is that you are leaping for. This book should serve as a tool to motivate, encourage and push you along the way. Whatever you are aspiring to obtain, it is possible. In five short but impactful chapters, I will explain how to wholeheartedly fulfill your intentions.

Now, let's prepare to help you find your purpose. Be an active reader. Take notes! Highlight where necessary and be sure to utilize the spaces provided to outline your strategy. I hope you are inspired to LIVE YOUR DREAM, too, once you reach the final chapter. Remember, it starts with a commitment.

Sincerely (with gratitude),

-LRW

Chapter One:

Believe in Yourself

This is probably the most cliché three-word directional in the history of reassuring advice. However, it's relevant. If you don't believe in yourself, who will?

Bookmark this page and take a look at the front cover. Examine it closely... My shirt displays the text: **Future Bestselling Author.** Now (re)read the bottom text: *UBAWA and Amazon Bestselling Author.* Before releasing my first book, *Amateur Thoughts: A Personal Collection of iWrite Poetry & LRW Quotes*, I declared that I would become a Bestselling Author by age 30. I accomplished that feat three years sooner than expected. This happened solely based on the fact that I believed in myself at the primary level, which propelled me to where I am today.

I stopped waiting for others to persuade my way of thinking by sharing their own failures and mistakes. Instead, I adjusted my state of mind through self-reflection, gradually, but permanently. Although it's logical to assume that patterns are repeated, it doesn't make sense for us to mimic someone else's path. We all have our own journeys to navigate. Furthermore, belief in oneself is evident when there is no hesitation in the midst of chance and opportunity.

When you believe in yourself, you will rarely pause or second-guess your abilities. Your instincts will guide you, and they won't steer you wrong.

Sacrifice always comes before success...
in life and in the dictionary. ~LRW

Are you willing to sacrifice for your goal(s)? Would you give up everyday necessities for the sake of happiness and fulfillment? Can you go a long while without experiencing the luxury of convenience? Strive to be content; not complacent.

I wake up in the middle of the night to respond to emails. That's IF I even fall asleep. Sometimes I skip breakfast, lunch and/or dinner because writing keeps me full. I'm always thinking about how I can make *iWrite4orU* bigger and better. When I'm working on one book, I'm brainstorming about the next one. I check my bank account daily, and my stagnant balance doesn't lead to stagnant effort. I breathe my brand!

There's something inside of you that only you can access. You must want it. Whatever "it" is... Grab it, grip it and grow it.

Who are you (beyond your given name)?

When did you start believing in yourself (honestly)?

What do you believe about yourself?

When did you start believing in yourself (honestly)?

Where did belief in yourself come from?

Why do you believe in yourself?

Chapter Two:
Create a Plan

"A goal without a plan is just a wish."

If you fail to plan, you plan to fail... You've read it, you've heard it, you've ignored it. No matter how spontaneous you may be, how much thrill you get from doing things on a whim, or how accustomed you are to putting things off, you must train your mind to work on a schedule. It's no different from how you train yourself to do other things that are equally important. Your goals should be a top priority, even when they are comfortably addressed last. The longer you wait, the harder it will be for you to execute your route to success. You control the outcome based on your effort, and creating a plan is the first step to achieving the desires of your heart. Draft ideas without forcing them to make sense. That's the motive for brainstorming. Ask questions. Seek answers.

Give in to the awareness and let it reveal what you can't naturally discern. You don't have to figure it all out in the beginning. And you won't. Be patient. Of course it will take a little time to narrow down what you are striving for. Rest assured that your ambition will heighten during this period.

Where do I start?

We are all born with talents and skills, but those talents and skills can lie dormant for years, especially if we suppress the urge to nurture them. That's why we're encouraged early on to identify our interest(s). Herein lies the overused yet compelling interrogative phrase: "What do you want to be when you grow up?"

Can you recall your response to that question, verbatim? You've more than likely neglected those premature hopes and aspirations. We never stop growing up. So, in retrospect, we should never stop planning and setting goals. With this particular mentality, move forward and embrace the things that make you unique. You have a specific calling. Everyone isn't introduced to their calling right away. Some even spend a lifetime searching for it, unsuccessfully. More often than not, one's calling is unveiled after much trial and error with various endeavors. Pay attention to what excites you. What arouses your spirit?

Define your objective and respect your deadline.

A hidden agenda is to an ulterior motive as a figure of speech is to a rhetorical question, and the Five Ws are a crucial subject when teaching the effective use of rhetoric. In most cases, a point cannot be proven without explaining Who, What, When, Where, and Why. Likewise, the Five Ws help rationalize any scenario by putting thoughts, feelings and actions in perspective.

Throughout the following consecutive chapters, you will notice my sly incorporation of the Five Ws; a manner of active reading. Context clues and such. I want you to be confident in your plan. Tweak it however you see fit so that it's personalized to convey exactly 1. **who** you are, 2. clearly state **what** your focus is, 3. tell me, yourself and the world **when** this plan will be accomplished (deadline), 4. **where** it will take you and 5. **why** it's such a big deal.

Plan around your passion(s) in pursuit of your purpose.

Many goal-setters get sidetracked or misdirected because they confuse the elements of a goal versus a dream. A goal is the standard. A dream is the target. In simple terms, the goal is the *how* in the line of who, what, when, where, and why events.

What separates goal-setters from dream-chasers?

One word: discipline. When you're chasing a dream, you may never catch up to it. Hence, my **LIVE YOUR DREAM** motto. If you dedicate every waking moment to doing what you love, the progressive amount of satisfaction is unmatched. And trust me, the struggle is worthwhile. Additionally, setting goals keeps you grounded in attainment, because you don't want to let yourself down.

Scene from Sister Act 2:

Whoopi Goldberg to Lauryn Hill: "I went to my mother who gave me this book called *Letters To A Young Poet* by Rainer Maria Rilke. He's a fabulous writer. A fellow used to write to him and say: I want to be a writer, please read my stuff. And Rilke says to this guy, Don't ask me about being a writer. If when you wake up in the morning you can think of nothing but writing, then you're a writer."

I'm a writer. I've known it since I was 12 years old. Originally, I didn't have a plan. I was more concerned about self-discovery and self-acceptance. Eventually, I had to begin treating my passion like it mattered in order to allow clearance for the inception of my dream. Look at me now...

I want you to have this same feeling of accomplishment, but you have to want it too. Your plan should be realistic. Don't embellish and start plotting for things that you know you can't handle physically, mentally or emotionally. If you are honest with yourself about what's feasible, your plan is guaranteed to manifest accordingly.

Again, who are you?

What is your plan? Explain the focus.

When will you accomplish your plan?

Where will your plan take you?

Why is your plan (proposal) such a big deal?

Chapter Three:
Stop Procrastinating

"You may delay, but time will not." – Benjamin Franklin

Do what you said you were going to do.

There's nothing worse than being discredited due to an inability to keep your word. Truth is the most common, uncommon entity. Yes, you read that correctly. Since we only get one chance to make a good, initial impression, lies have no room to escalate. Doing what you said you were going to do is not always easy. Whether the deficiency is blamed on forgetfulness or disregard for someone else's existence, as well as your own, neither is a valid excuse. Back up your claims with action and speak with movement.

Before you can gain support when it comes to reaching a goal, you must make it known that you are trustworthy. Keep this in mind:

Procrastination generates unreliability.

When I was in the process of writing my novel, *Dearly Beloved S.I.S.T.A.S*, not only was I frantic about meeting my final deadline, I was also unsure about how I would be able to fund the project. But, I believed in myself and I had a plan.

The next order of business was to stop procrastinating and do what I said I was going to do: release it in the summer of 2013.

Only a few people can share details concerning the type of pressure I was under. Fortunately, I work best when deadlines are near. With the burden of fixing unexpected car problems and the responsibility of paying unwavering bills, I had to find a way to get my future bestseller in the hands of the public, on time. After consulting with some friends and colleagues, I was informed about Kickstarter: a crowdfunding platform that is utilized to launch all sorts of creative projects. In 30 days, 109 backers pledged $5,230, allowing me to surpass my initial $5,000 goal. Many of them were strangers, or individuals that I had no real connection to, other than our interaction on social media. The power of networking...

Because of their faith in me and the impact I had made on their lives somehow, I was able to do what I said I was going to do. This can be applied in multiple instances. However, you shouldn't develop a habit of relying on others to assist you with following through. Be accountable for your own promises and declarations.

While writing this book, I stumbled across this message in social media land: *Your purpose is not what you do to bring home a paycheck.* I agree 100%.

Too many people are obsessed with the notion of surviving, and not enough people are obsessed with actually living.

Don't Make Excuses, Be the Exception.

I can't live my dream (yet) because...

I'm a single mother.
I have too many bills.
No one will support me.
I tried once and failed.
It won't pay me enough.
I don't have the time.
It's too late.

Pick an objection, or add another. Neither will suffice for the lack of commitment on display. Get rid of the apprehension. You owe it to yourself!

New year, different pledge, same conclusion.

Every year, we all come up with New Year's resolutions that tend to fade quite rapidly. A new year's resolution is an instant choice of change, but change isn't an instant thing. That's why goals must be set. They hold more weight. Remember my section on dreams vs. goals? When you set out to achieve something at the same time every year, it creates a never-ending cycle of defensive reasoning.

Since you are not held responsible for failing at the liabilities you place upon yourself, it's easier to avoid the repercussions of the end result.

Earlier this year, I decided to break down my ultimate resolution into mini goals, as a method of creating something tangible that I'm indebted to. I first began setting mini goals that complemented my big goals on a day-to-day basis. Then, I revisited those goals to assess if I was on track or not. Here's part of my January mini goal data:

January 1, 2014
Big Goal: Sell 5,000 Books Independently
Small Goal: Sell 15 eBooks and 5 Paperbacks
(All Titles Included) – Partly Accomplished

January 2, 2014
Big Goal: Maintain Health and Increase Energy
Small Goal: Run 2 miles/100 squats after work
Success w/ Substitution - Insanity (45 Minutes)

January 3, 2014
Big Goal: $5000 in Business Savings by Dec. 31
Small Goal: Pay rent and save what's left.
Failed - Splurged on dinner and a movie

January 4, 2014
Big Goal: Don't waste time.
Small Goal: Refuse sleeping in.

Success - Attended "At the Table" event, sold three books and made beneficial connections, which helped secure three future January appearances.

January 5, 2014
Invite three guests to church - Accomplished

January 6, 2014
Pause #WriterGrind. DO NOT touch laptop. Relax and cheer on the NOLES! - Accomplished

January 7, 2014
Update performance/appearance résumé and work on press kit. – Still in Progress

January 8, 2014
Write a new blog post for #WriterWednesday
Accomplished – "He Mrs. Me"

January 9, 2014
Cook dinner... Find a new recipe to try.
Accomplished – Salmon & Asparagus

January 10, 214
Go on an "interesting" date. - Accomplished

January 11, 2014
Sell 10 books.
Accomplished - Sold 9 Paperbacks and 1 eBook.

January 12, 2014
Rest and Relaxation - Accomplished

January 13, 2014
Don't skip breakfast. Drink 4-6 bottles of water.
Partly Accomplished - Ate a banana and drank three bottles of water.

January 14, 2014
Follow up with new contacts from networking events I've attended this month. – Accomplished

January 15, 2014
Write a new poem. - Accomplished later.

January 16, 2014
Reach 1,000 "Likes" on iWrite4orU company page. Accomplished at a later date.

January 17, 2014
Date night with my Date Knight. His choice. My treat. – Accomplished

January 18, 2014
Sell 15 Books @ E3 Book Publishers' Day. Recruit two first-time authors. – Partly Accomplished (Sold 9 books. Met one prospective author.)

January 19, 2014
Schedule Facebook iWrite4orU posts for the week Accomplished

January 20, 2014
Register for One Spark – Deterred until next year.

January 21, 2014
Create all #WriterWednesday social media posts for 1/22 – Accomplished.

January 22, 2014
Wake up at 5:00am and write chapter summaries for LIVE YOUR DREAM: How to Set and Accomplish Deadline-Driven Goals - Accomplished

January 23, 2014
Run 2 miles before work - Failed

January 24, 2014
Complete edits on latest iWrite4orU Manuscript. – Accomplished

January 25, 2014
Finish Press Kit – Partly Accomplished

A temporary failure does not correspond with an eternal loss. – LRW

Monitoring your mini goals intensely will prompt you to stretch so far that you will exceed your own expectations in the end.

Write down everything you want to accomplish this week (on Sunday), whether it's pertaining to your dream or other responsibilities, and mark the failure/success ratio on the coming Saturday. As the next week approaches, determine which factors prevented you from effectively completing the goals you set the week before. Every week is a fresh start, but don't take it for granted.

Who are you trying to impress?

What is it that you said you were going to do?

When did you say you were going to do it?

Where will you end up once you do what you said were going to do?

Why haven't you done what you said you were going to do yet?

Chapter Four:

Eliminate the Fear

"The only thing we have to fear is fear itself."
– Franklin D. Roosevelt

You've probably seen the word FEAR decoded as the acronym, False. Evidence. Appearing. Real... but do you totally understand what that means? Fear cripples us all, even when we think we've defeated it. It's a natural emotion; one that isn't easy to conceal. Only a blind man can proclaim not to be afraid of things that are invisible. Does that make sense? When you're faced with challenges, you won't always be armed and prepared for battle. These are the times when weaknesses make themselves known. So how do you eliminate the fear? By fighting it with poise and maintaining a high volume of stability. Fear usually creeps up when you are vulnerable and unsure. Be certain about your goals! You're destined to become an undisputed champion of great deeds. Besides, the more aggressive you are, the more fragile fear becomes. Break the curse with persistence. Also, stop wasting time and energy trying to create a Plan B.

If you're contemplating a Plan B, you're giving fear an open invitation to stunt your odds, which can fester into a hazard that kills your advancement. Like any disruption, it affects routine and causes you to rewind. Your dream has to be the main focus, mainly when things are unclear.

Fear and doubt cannot win... not ever!

Who are you when fear isn't present?

Who are you when fear isn't present?

What is your personal concept of fear?

When does fear bother you the most?

Where do you think you would be if fear didn't exist?

Why are you allowing fear to hold you back?

Chapter Five:

Trust God

"Trust in the LORD with all your heart and lean not on your own understanding; in all your ways acknowledge Him, and He will make your paths straight."

– Proverbs 3:5-6

You may not be religious, spiritual or an adamant believer, but know this: God is real. I can testify to a multitude of blessings, none based on luck or random fortune. I won't oversaturate this chapter with my personal beliefs. In fact, I'll just impart some truth for you to absorb and do with it what you will... I was baptized at age 13, without full comprehension of the act of worship. I just knew that religion was an understood practice in my family and I was expected to obey. At that age, I practically had no choice. As I grew older, experienced some heartache and seemingly failed at most things I tried to govern myself, I still had no choice. God kept showing up and showing out, and I desperately wanted to take all the credit.

Some unknown individual has been quoted for stating, "I'd rather live my life believing God exists and die finding out He doesn't than live as if He doesn't and die finding out He does."

I was never a non-believer; but I can admit to being a redeemed non-acknowledger. Although I was instructed to pray often since birth, I unfortunately strayed away from that command during the latter portion of my teen years. Nevertheless, the intimate conversations that I have with God these days fuel and orchestrate my progression.

Regardless of any advice I have received or may soon receive from those who have survived countless downfalls, my trust in Him is what I depend on when deciding to commit to any venture. Case in point, when I was pondering the pros and cons of quitting my job, I was continually advised to "wait on God." But what was I waiting for? No apparent sign was going to fall from the sky and He would not appear as an imaginary, fictional character to deliver the message face-to-face. Our souls are overflowing with conviction, but most of us stubbornly sit back and anticipate some form of clarity instead of trusting that God's got us from the get-go... no ifs, ands or buts about it.

In conclusion, please take heed to all that's been previously mentioned and live your dream, before it dies, unbothered and untouched. You'll forever regret it if you don't.

Goal-Setting Tips: (Strict Deadlines Required)

"R" you ready to LIVE YOUR DREAM?

Reminders - Display your goals in frequented, noticeable places: the calendar or notes section on your smartphone, refrigerator door, bathroom mirror, dashboard of your car, etc.

Relationships - Bond with like-minded individuals, solicit help from a mentor, ask a loved one or significant other for their honest input.

Royalties - Pay yourself with time before even thinking about paying yourself with money. If you're working a 9 to 5, value your downtime (between 12 to 9 and 5 to 12). Rest is necessary, but sleep is optional. Use the floating hours wisely.

Records - Progress is only a slow process if you aren't examining how far you've advanced. Every time you make a stride with your goals, file it for reflective, motivational keeping.

Rewards - You have so much to gain when you finally decide to LIVE YOUR DREAM. No amount of compensation will ever be enough once you get the hang of your purpose. Freedom is a priceless prize. **Reap** what you sow.

Acknowledgements

They say "third time's a charm", but the fourth time around is just as lovely. Words cannot express how thankful I am, but I'll use them to indicate my appreciation anyway. God has been better to me than I've been to myself and others combined. I am not always worthy of His blessings, so I cherish my gift the best way I know how... by utilizing it to make a difference and to inspire change. I never thought I'd be able to be this much of an influence. I just wanted to be somebody... somebody important to the people of the world... and somebody that my parents could be proud of. Mom and Dad, I can't thank you both enough for your constant support and for loving me unconditionally, not as a duty, but as a privilege, never lacking to make me feel significant. My brother, Terrell: You give me a reason to push harder and be better. I know that you are often looking my way for guidance and expecting me to set a positive example. I won't ever let you down. My close family and friends, clients and associates, and especially my faithful readers and true supporters: Thank you to infinity, beyond and back! Mr. KL, I love you. You've given my #WriterGrind™ a whole new meaning...

–LRW

Author's Bio

Born and raised in Jacksonville, Florida, Liltera R. Williams (LRW) fell in love with writing at age 12 and married it at 18. From the moment she began penciling down thoughts and ideas in her first diary, and then formally learning how to compose essays and pieces of fiction during her high school and college years, she knew that she would someday have an opportunity to share her gift with the world. Her given name was perhaps a foreshadowing of the future works she would produce to establish herself in history as a Literary Trailblazer. After graduating from Florida State University in December of 2008, LRW set out to build her professional writing portfolio by pitching stories and carrying out reporting assignments for various publications. She is now well-known as a Motivational Poet, Devoted Freelance Writer, Skilled Editor and Bestselling Author (Amazon & UBAWA: Urban Books Authors and Writers of America).

In addition to having articles published in Jacksonville Magazine, 904 Magazine, EU Jacksonville Newspaper, The Ponte Vedra Recorder, The First Coast Register and Sister2Sister Magazine, her published catalog includes: Amateur Thoughts: A Personal Collection of iWrite Poetry & LRW Quotes (*Amazon Bestseller*), Dearly Beloved S.I.S.T.A.S (*UBAWA Top 100 Books of 2013*), Words from the Write Side of My Heart, LIVE

YOUR DREAM: How to Set and Accomplish Deadline-Driven Goals, and soon-to-come releases, Spelling B (Children's Book) and Date Knight: A Man Who Findeth A Wife (Novel).

In the process of developing her inspirational LIVE YOUR DREAM movement and expanding her entrepreneurial knowledge, LRW originated a unique term to define her purpose—#WriterGrind™: a strategic quest to accomplish various writing objectives while striving to conquer the demands of authorship. She believes that anything is possible with the determined mindset of Effort, Perseverance and Faith. In LRW's own words, "If you're living without giving, your talents are null and void."

www.ingramcontent.com/pod-product-compliance
Lightning Source LLC
Chambersburg PA
CBHW071745020426
42331CB00008B/2177